BIG MAD!

By T'Arrah Marjé
ILLUSTRATED BY CAMERON WILSON

To my beautiful and brave little sisters: Situations are not always as hard as they might seem. Remember to take your time. Close your eyes and open your mind. Listen to your heart and feel your soul. Don't allow the situation to take control. You take control of the situation through prayer and meditation.

My name is Kennie Beans, but don't look at me because I'm big mad! This morning I didn't get my way, and that made things bad for the rest of my day. Mom gave me cereal for breakfast when I wanted cake. That made my mood bad.

The rest of the day things got worse on the ride to school with Dad. I had forgotten to tie my shoe laces.

In class I didn't have much patience. The teacher taught, but I didn't care. It was her own time she was wasting; because today I'm big mad! I'm not in a good mood. I don't even care to get a new attitude.

During lunch I tried to pass through. I guess the other kids didn't see me, so I just yelled, "MOVE!" I didn't mean to be so rude. Today I wish I was at another school.

At recess, well, I couldn't play. I had to finish my test, because I didn't pay attention earlier today. Therefore, inside the classroom I had to stay. I hate not getting my way. I ended up failing the test anyway.

Then I heard my teacher say to me, "Kennie Beans, you're having a big bad day I see."
She was right. I couldn't have a big good day if it was in plain sight.

"Let me tell you something that someone once told me. The energy we put out is what comes back. You see?"

I didn't understand, so I asked her to say it again. "It means people and things around us sometime respond better to us when we approach them in a better mood. Also remember, everything doesn't go our way all the time, and that's fine. However, it shouldn't stop us from being kind or nice to ourselves or others."

She was right. This morning I didn't have to get upset with my mother. I just was frustrated, and that I hated.

"Maybe tomorrow you should start your day with a little meditation."

"MEDICATION?!?!?!"

"No silly, meditation."

"How do I do that?"

"Thinking in peace and focusing on your breathing is where it's at."

The next morning I took the time to meditate. By sitting with my thoughts and slowly breathing inside and out, I closed my eyes and imagined all the things my day would be about. I inhaled the happy thoughts and exhaled the bad ones. I thought of all the ways today that I'd like to have fun.

Yesterday I learned that sometimes our day can be overwhelming, but with a little meditation, the day can be astounding! Today I'll be patient. Today I'll take my time. It feels good to leave a bad attitude behind.

When I handle things with a better mood, toward other kids I wasn't rude. I listened in class, and guess what? This time on my test I passed! Things even worked out better with Mom and Dad. Oh, you can look at me now, because I'm no longer big mad.

Made in the USA
Columbia, SC
22 September 2021